VIVISECTION

❦

ERIC WEINSTEIN

VIVISECTION

ERIC WEINSTEIN

NEW MICHIGAN PRESS
TUCSON, ARIZONA

NEW MICHIGAN PRESS
DEPT OF ENGLISH, P. O. BOX 210067
UNIVERSITY OF ARIZONA
TUCSON, AZ 85721-0067

<http://newmichiganpress.com/nmp>

Orders and queries to nmp@thediagram.com.

Copyright © 2010 by Eric Weinstein.
All rights reserved.

ISBN 978-1-934832-25-7. FIRST PRINTING.

Printed in the United States of America.

Design by Ander Monson.

Cover art: © Andrei Calangiu | Dreamstime.com.

CONTENTS

Copula 1
Anatomy Lesson (I) 3
Diagnosis 4
Persistence of Memory 6
Jovian Sky 8
Ho*e (I) 10
Field Notes 12
A Satellite Sees into Your Heart 15
Golem 17
Anatomy Lesson (II) 19
Persephone's Telephone 20
Open Heart Surgery 22
Live! from the Mariana Trench 24
Ho*e (II) 26
Directions to Lake Bonneville 28
Panel on Borderland 30
Donor 32
Anatomy Lesson (III) 34
Letter to Allen, 2:12 AM 36
Ho*e (III) 37
Surrender Dorothy 39
Transmission from Isthmus Connecting Tongue
    and Subconscious 41
Anatomy Lesson (IV) 43

CONTENTS

Short Program   44
Ho*e (IV)   46
Repercussions of the Arecibo Message   48
New Theories in Human Life Extension   50
After Adam   52

Notes & Acknowledgments   55

for Ian

COPULA

    Narcissus arrived alive
& the bird did not.

    A motorcycle accident:
they collided at 70 miles

    an hour, the dead wren lodged
in his chest over the heart. Listen,

    he said, it must have mistaken
me for a mirror, or a window—

    seeing in me itself & nothing,
it was entranced, as I have been

    by the stream, days at a time.
He slept then, & the doctors

    worked. Like a pregnant woman
or conjoined twins, man and bird

    were seraphim, if only
for an hour: two hearts,

    one form. & like mother from
child, brother from brother, rent

from one another, the small
beak is pried from the flesh

& the flesh closed up after.
Listen, Narcissus said, awake,

aging is a series of glass doors
closing behind you, like

windows—but before he
could finish, one doctor,

still intent on the wren, was
offering the stethoscope like

an infant: There is a heartbeat,
a heartbeat, he was saying, Listen.

ANATOMY LESSON (I)

Note the dark concavity of the skull.
    (Inside it the night is very long.)

The architecture of the inner ear
    a marvel: hammer & anvil, hammering

away in the long night. Here is the heart
    with six wings (fig. *b*). Primordial

dragonfly, it hovers all day over water (remember
    that water, like all things, casts a shadow).

See here the shadows of the ribs
    over the lungs: thin, insisting,

rungs of a bowed ladder folding
    like wind into night, into longing, into night.

DIAGNOSIS

I have an unhealthy attraction
to hospitals.

I come in and unbutton my shirt,
insist that something is wrong with me,

beat on the triage nurse's desk,
on the glass door to the trauma unit.

Four hours later I am informed
there are pieces missing,

whole organs, removed like batteries,
and yet my blood still moves.

The doctors wash in and out.
Lub-dub. Lub-dub.

E pur. E pur.
(And yet. And yet.)

Four days later, at my kitchen table
the phone rings.

Good news, they say. You're missing
just four chambers of your heart,

four base pairs in your DNA
(adenine, thymine, cytosine, guanine),

at most four fingers from each hand.
—Oh yes, the facts are in

and you can live without your heart.
(We have machines for that.)

PERSISTENCE OF MEMORY

You bury a light bulb in the yard
& grow a blown glass tree.

It's all your parents talk about
for hours after you've gone to sleep.

By morning the branches are hung
with tungsten leaves. The neighbors

complain because it attracts lightning,
even though it glows like an echo-

cardiogram for hours after each strike.
You are asleep when your father rakes

a chainsaw across the trunk, but the sound
carries & you wake, you run out, shouting

I'll never forgive you, not ever. Of course you do,
hours later. A persistent cough carries you

to the emergency room, or rather, your father does.
They remove a filament from your tongue,

a spun glass feather from your trachea.
There were never any birds, your mother says.

The fiberoptic bronchoscope proves
otherwise: they find a miniature light

bulb, glass sapling, copper wire nest
& remove them from your lung.

Imagine that, the doctors say, voices
carrying through the anesthesia.

Imagine that, your mother says, so you do,
or rather, you remember your tree.

It's all the surgical team talks about
for hours while you're asleep.

It's all the surgical team talks about
for hours after you've gone home.

JOVIAN SKY

> *At certain altitudes, it is believed to have a blue sky.*
> —from an encyclopedia article, "Jupiter"

It couldn't be the only
one, our sky, we knew this:
the alchemy of metals into worlds
was not unique.

(Galileo knew the Talmud
knew even the Egyptians
knew their mud their bricks
were nothing new, an earth
was nothing new.) Created?
Yes, in multitudes. An atmosphere for each.

Some believe that after building
atomic nuclei, chlorophyll, grief,
God, seeing he was still alone,
killed himself.
You will have no other gods.
This was not meant for you.

Much later, after we developed
leavened bread, penicillin, lunar modules,
we could hear this clearly. Collectively
the skies of the universe murmured

words they murmured
Icarus. Hindenburg.

Occasionally they shear the wings off
space shuttles, let go of a Boeing,
obliterate a satellite to remind us:
Earth's is blue, and others are blue; those
are no more yours than this one.
We were not meant for you.

We know this. Still, in the evenings
we hollow our bones like the ancestors of birds.

HO*E (I)

BOSTON, MASSACHUSETTS, 2006

I remembered the water
& I thought it was deep—

deep like holes
dug to China, like

presumably Marx. The spot
with an x on

it: written in oil, the spot
of earth blood

on the proverbial carpet.
The site of fratricide, of

a pigeon pecking
at a pigeon's corpse

before the depression
could fill with rain.

I carried the memory
for years unmodified,

like electromagnetic
relics committed

to the Internet's infinite
memory: a hole of small fires

in which nothing changes.
A manuport. I thought

I remembered a lake
& found the city pool,

had forgotten: the dead
pigeon endlessly pecked by

its brother, ever disappearing
into a hole in the air.

FIELD NOTES

I.

The first time I did it
improperly—no sand, only
water & salt. Later

I added fractured
quartz, snail shells. I
set it all up in the bathtub:

gull feathers, driftwood,
six fish, brine shrimp, a tiny
Titanic (shipwrecks being

a good source of iron). I
roused waves by making
love in said shipwreck.

II.

Birds are easier: few
feathers, little clockwork,
a key to wind them up.

Crow turns back & forth
in his tree. Parrot repeats
what parrot will: *escape*.

The simple one dips
& drinks from the glass,
dips: drinks: drips: repeats.

III.

Volcanoes are problematic
in that they require virgins.
Years ago, only baking soda

& vinegar, but no longer.
I started mine at the bottom
of the sea. I know little

of seamounts or supercritical fluids.
Seamount: noun: merman or -maid.
Supercritical fluid: noun: blood, or

any liquid transmitting life
and death. When the volcano died
I slept on the cooling pillow lava.

IV.

I have a heart & so I know
how to make one. It is no
secret: human beings are one

part malice, four parts glass,
four glass rooms in space
subtracted from one lung.

Imagine an aquarium, bright
fish, only the kinds that kill
one another. Better yet,

imagine the kinds that are
transparent, you can see
their hearts going. Imagine

fish within fish hearts within fish.
Imagine that girl in the shipwreck
was your mother, no mermaid.

A SATELLITE SEES INTO YOUR HEART

after Dan Chiasson

A satellite sees into your heart
& registers a minor tremor, toy earthquake.

A satellite sees into your heart,
mistaking the transplant scar for a fault.

A satellite sees into your heart,
sees your home but not your hometown.

A satellite sees into your heart
& recognizes itself in the reflection.

A satellite sees into your heart
like a starling sees into your chimney.

A satellite sees into your heart,
sees a blood puzzle it cannot solve.

A satellite sees into your heart
& like Osiris, weighs it, finds it wanting.

A satellite sees into your heart,
discovers the meaning of the word *artificial*.

A satellite sees into your heart
& inadvertently sets it on fire.

A satellite sees into your heart
& wants it, haunted or not.

A satellite sees into your heart.
A satellite sees into your heart.

GOLEM

When you left for a week
I added teeth forged from bone,
coal-fired, fossilized, formed

from the horns of a triceratops.
As for the bones themselves: wood,
burnt & polished, furnished when

you said *this isn't working*. I was working,
fashioning faces from bullet casings,
possible eyes from black volcanic

glass, a modern-day Vulcan. The day
you left for good, it grew as tall as the room
(in truth, I'd burnt the baby

grand & mixed the ashes with
old dishwater for more clay).
They say these chimeras

are mute by nature, though
this one would sit in the bathroom
all night, echoing the sound

of dripping fixtures (my fault
for adding parrot feathers,
a howler monkey's heart). & yes,

I could have erased the *truth*
burnt into its forehead, left
only *death* and it would

have listened. I could have built
thirty birdhouses from the body.
—No, not really. The truth is,

I'd designed a device to recite
my vices. It needed a voice.
I gave it yours.

ANATOMY LESSON (II)

All day the brain's leaky faucet
    drips in its darkened apartment,

dampened chords echoing
    down the halls of the spinal canal.

Measureless, measureless,
    measureless,

it is a wonder the lower organs
    never drown.

PERSEPHONE'S TELEPHONE

is, naturally, in the kitchen, next to four human hearts
she keeps in a jar labeled EARTHQUAKES that is always
breaking itself. No small surprise the underworld is
populated chiefly by smoke & ice sculptures *i.e.* ghosts.
When it rings, Persephone answers & they shatter. Her
breath smells like air inside a plastic bag. Not deathly,
per se. Phone calls to birds, like so: *tweet tweet tweet*. &
they follow. The feed: human bone meal & pomegranate
seeds. What else to eat underground?

Coughing, chthonically ill, she sweeps debris into
the Styx, the glass, the salt waters & seals her hearts
in a new jar labeled FUGUES. Sometimes she finds
strangers on the line, asking after late husbands, siblings
presumed over, the occasional telemarketer selling life
insurance. Orpheus calls at least once a week, asking for
the impossible way back.

When she was a girl, before she knew death, she built
bottled ships with her father. *Remember*, Hades cautions
when she returns late each autumn, *ships break & hearts
leak*. Charon bails brine from his iron ferry, breaks the
ice always forming over & over the Styx.

Persephone stands at the counter, absorbing her hearts'
salt dissolved. Below her, in the cellar, Hades opens

bag after bag of salvaged glass, rebuilding her jars &
ordering them on the shelf, an alphabet of loss: *a* is for
ACCIDENTS, *b* is for BLAME, & so on. On the upstairs
telephone Persephone listens to the dial tone. It sounds
like birds singing, tinnitus. The new jar falls beneath
her private sky of roots & buried power lines, reflecting
her face as she remembers that morning she was stolen,
driven deep into the hidden rooms of the Earth.

OPEN HEART SURGERY

An hour later, her blood diverted,
her heart stops and the machines take over.

(He scrubs his arms to the elbows.
He is her surgeon and husband
of twenty-eight years.)

He cuts through her pericardium,
a fiery sword,
a flowering garden.
(They say in heaven
there are no husbands and no wives.)

Against the humming of equipment
he thinks of another time,
winter, many years ago
his ear pressed to her chest
on the couch in her college apartment.

That night, he had dreamed
white worlds slept beneath her skin.

After they close her up,
successful, he does not think
of bright white skies or complications.

Only this:

that her heart,
pale and still as a stone in water,
had looked just like every other.

LIVE! FROM THE MARIANA TRENCH

Tonight I will take my bathysphere
to the deepest reach of the sea.

I will take with me a plate
of sandwiches and a copy

of *Sgt. Pepper's Lonely Hearts Club Band*
on vinyl. And I will eat and play

"Lucy in the Sky with Diamonds"
for all the whales and shrimp and

diatomaceous folk and they will say,
Fuck yes, what is this sky thing, what

are diamonds, they sound awesome,
and I will say, Yes, they are pretty

awesome. And when they ask what
the sky and diamonds are like, I will say

They are like you, sparkling in the dark,
waiting for the next song to start.

And when they ask who Lucy is,
I will tell them she was my mother

in a way, but she's dead, she died
millions of years ago in Ethiopia.

And they will say, You are like her.
And I will say Yes, but unlike her I am live!

From the Mariana Trench, and I will be
here all night, is there anything you want

to hear, is there anything I can trade for
your whale song before I have to return

to the overworld, before I run out of air,
before I go off the air, before I go home?

HO*E (II)

INDIANAPOLIS, INDIANA, 1949

for Kurt Vonnegut

I believe the green light inside
the photocopier & escalator are the same,

some lesser saint in shirt-sleeves living
under the stairs, turning out duplicates

two by two, up & down, like that
octogenarian & his zoo-boat, herding

pairs of coyotes, ghost orchids, wasps
in their paper nests, driving them up

& up into the boat as it hove, down
& down into the hold. (Stay. Good dog.) But o—

how long before the green dawn broke?
Who ate whom during those forty nights?

& was the patron saint of Xerox there? You
know, if so, he would have kept a record:

the *zap-zap* of the wasps in the hive,
rain walking around upstairs like bombs,

sheet after wasp-paper sheet reaching up
to the boy with his magnifying glass.

DIRECTIONS TO LAKE BONNEVILLE

for Laura

Lock your keys in the car. Leave
your cell phone behind, there is
no signal here. As for yourself, own

nothing, or nearly. Carry only what's needed:
a branch to walk with, some lunch.
An apple maybe, and a knife.

Shed a year for each step you take. The lake
is old, can only be reached by going back,
never forward. Think back, then, go back, swim

back: wade out waist deep in the water,
keep your clothes if you like. Watch
the sky. The summer rains are coming.

Remember: an eye is a salt lake reflecting
the lake. Light swims in each. The lake
evaporates and refills with rain. Look,

there's Theseus on the shore, building and
rebuilding. There's Odysseus among the sirens,
his heart a salt lake reflecting the lake,

the women in white dresses so bright
they make your eyeballs ache. Remember
hearts break and ships leak, but shed

no tears: meet me at Lake Bonneville.
The heart is a salt lake reflecting.
In the eye the wide world turns.

PANEL ON BORDERLAND

Dear tightrope walker, dear man
praying in the Port Authority terminal,
dear terminal man: all of you
will go down to the earth one day,
one-way street & dead end, past
hatchets calcified, palindromes hewn
from each tree: bare limbs reflecting
roots in the black earth,
initials carved in each trunk. Past
deep snow, wolf bones, through
the dismantled world-after
the earth keeps in cold
storage—o it will never surrender
your dead dog, your father, my
father, anyone's father—dear
Centralia: will you never cease? Everything
burning in a box underground, coal
mostly, though also relatives, fossilized
hearts, composted valentines, half-composed
symphonies, decomposed monks. Dear
ferryman crossing the Hudson: how
do you know when you've exchanged
one state for another, & what
is the toll? Dear Charon:
same question. A fall is a fall
whether a season, in love, or passing

from a great height—hallowed
the way rot hollows a tree,
the way asphalt sanctifies
gravity, its improbable lines of force
invisible as grief, the Equator.

DONOR

CHRISTMAS, 1979

Your corneas taken first. Next, the twin cathedrals
of your lungs exhumed—red heart—dark liver—

the tree lit up like an angiogram, some branches
half-vanished, night dilating into the empty

space: a map of the underworld written in air
with the thin, starry opalescence of a chest x-ray.

Your kidneys mined from the deepest regions of
the self, now bloodless, nearly weightless, & you

no longer magnetic, no longer tied to the earth's
spinning fields, ten billion years of iron—rust—

the transubstantiated carbon hulls of stars,
ferrous wheels of meteors extracted. Pyrrhic

victory, your life grafted to so many others,
scattered farther than ashes, like that impossible ash

tree of Norse mythology, reaching into everyone:
your heart laboring inside a new mother,

your lungs in two war veterans. An ironwood forest
deep as the wood from which we pulled

the Christmas tree, felled so suddenly, like you,
like a so-called act of God: here the cathedral, there the meteor.

ANATOMY LESSON (III)

The last man in the oncology ward
    brings daffodils to the mother
of a premature daughter.

She does not wake. Next door
    the boy with the disintegrating spine
falls asleep while praying. His sister

believes he will not die, & the last
    man, too, believes he will not die.
Outside the hallways bend like spoons.

The early daughter is too new to believe
    anything, or not to. The sister & brother,
mother & man believe many things,

anything: that radiation will remain
    effective, & so will marriage.
That there are over ten thousand saints.

The mother dreams field after mirrored field.
    The boy dreams of an orchard of bone.
The last man imagines a great salt lake

evaporated overnight. He believes this to be impossible. Several stories above, Saint Jude records the only known fact about mankind:

We would believe everything, if we only could.

LETTER TO ALLEN, 2:12 AM

Tonight it rains over New York & the sky is rust—
you never told me that, Allen, that night's machinery
could rust—now the starry dynamo ground to a halt,
now everything wound down the way time lapses over
mattresses no one sleeps on. I guess entropy's got to eat,
too—eat the crystal singing heavenly spheres like eggs cracking
up the way your mother did, the way all mothers do—
& I think I hear wolves, Allen, which are not indigenous
to my apartment any more than horse skeletons are indigenous
to the earth behind barns but still belong. I would have liked
to hear that hydrogen jukebox. To never see this sodium sky
again, this iron sky, orange as war: that's what it is, Allen. Iron & salt.
So is blood, ask anyone. I'd just like the sky to clear, Allen, so I
can get some sleep. To dream tonight I'm back in my childhood
home. To eat an egg in the kitchen's silence. To colonize the night's
labyrinthine spine. To sit in the attic & carve out the wish-bones of stars.

HO*E (III)

PATERSON, NEW JERSEY, 1986

for Oscar Wao

The rain tattooing the roof,
the wolf turning inside
out by the door,

the limited miracle of self-
trepanation: uneasy
before surgery,

the wolf inside opening
the wolf outside,
vivisection,

like Metallo & his kryptonite
heart—vicious gift—
radioactive.

You've got to bury that shit
far under the house
or poison

(was auch soll ein Gift machen?)
everyone—New Jersey
or not. Bury it,

even one ventricle, brain
or heart, x marking
the spot:

wolf chewing his thin want
bone, little more than
a cinder,

the problem of eroding still
insoluble, the digging
sisyphean.

SURRENDER DOROTHY

Today I will build an electric self-
contained heart. It will resemble
that sculpture by the Philadelphia
Wireman with its aortic nail
jutting out the side. It will be coin-
operated and run at the low price
of twenty-five cents per day. I
will collect the quarters from every-
one on a weekly basis and use them
to support orphans in far-flung
countries. One morning Robert
Jarvik and Sally Struthers will come
to my house and demand to know
how I did it. I will tell them, Mostly
by watching *The Wizard of Oz*
and Mr. Wizard. They will weep
with joy and ask for the schematics,
and I will say, Sleep first, or it won't
make sense. When they lie down
on my couch and enter the small
spinning house of sleep, I will go
into the kitchen and fill a tin cup
with water in preparation for the
lecture I'll deliver when they wake.
Outside the sorry noir door of the
house, the Tin Man will be listening,

tin hand cupped to tin ear, poised
to emboss my secret on his chest.

TRANSMISSION FROM ISTHMUS
CONNECTING TONGUE AND SUBCONSCIOUS

I am terrified of the flesh
eating virus peeling human
beings like oranges. I also fear

baby ghosts. I do not want
to see my friends even though
I like most of them and feel

OK. I do want to be a zoo
keeper or else an astronaut,
something involving contact

with non-humans, even aliens.
Humans are known reservoirs
of viruses, babies, or both. Also

probably ghosts. No wonder
I would like a new geography,
a strait into outer space or a

canal to navigate. Something
straightforward. Dog eating
smaller dog. Kangaroo bearing

new kangaroo. And that's
what gets me about the flesh
eating virus, the baby ghost:

Who is eating whom, flesh
and virus? Is it the ghost of a
baby, or the baby of a ghost?

ANATOMY LESSON (IV)

All morning I sank my teeth
in the east river—

bicuspid, incisor, molar,
molar. When they were gone

I moved on to heart valves, then
amino acids. By the time I reached *valine*

the water & the sky were dark.
I unhinged myself where it made sense:

the jaw, the manifold channels
of the palm, the arteries & veins

split bright open. I washed out
into the river, dismantling, listening

to the current's psalms, my blood's low hymn:
to water   *to water*
     to water   *to water*

SHORT PROGRAM

The knife balanced for years
between the hemispheres
of my brain will one day

slip & sever the name
of my own brother from
all memory. One day

the knife carefully sealed
in my cardiac walls
will chisel a clot from

my blood, long water-clock,
& the knife hanging in
the stairwell of the spine,

each microscopic knife
swinging gently on each
cellular pendulum

will strike, will catch in the
engine of me, the smell
of rain & gasoline—

& I, insomniac
in the kitchen cutting
artichoke hearts alone

or driving through darkness
to the all-night diner
will smell something burning,

mistime the bright panic
of the knife, of the deer
in the headlights: lightning

in the room like a struck
match, then everything blown
to cinders, long thunder:

& outside the window,
the sound of the darkness
undisturbed, still ticking.

HO*E (IV)

CENTRALIA, PENNSYLVANIA, 1979

> *Gott läßt sich nicht wie leichter Morgen leben.*
> *Wer einfährt in den Schacht, der hat der vollen*
> *Erde gefühl um Werkschaft aufzugeben:*
> *Der steht gebückt und lockert ihn im Stollen.*
> —Rainer Maria Rilke

If only I could bioluminesce.
If only my mouthful of smoke

weren't smoke, but cold light.
The trees bright with ice,

the smell of boiling Polaroid,
burnt letters from an old flame:

the world breaks slowly.
I trek into the abyss & replace

a light bulb, a sign of human
existence, a mine tour

of one—ghost town dissolving
in the subarachnoid space,

thread unwinding in the concave
darkness, shuffled mortal coal.

The streetlights extinguished
at six. The world is frozen closed

this time of year, I had to break
the locks on its doors to get in.

Down the hall & never right nor
left to that pine bedroom door. Behind:

the Minotaur, like death or Kennedy,
reads by the light of gunfire.

REPERCUSSIONS OF THE ARECIBO MESSAGE

Sometimes I imagine my spine
is a tuning fork, bifurcating
beneath my shoulder blades,
broadcasting my thoughts at
the resonant frequencies of
water, my principle component.

Sometimes I imagine a migration
of birds inside me, a migraine
showing me the lightning strike
of my own retinas, storm crows,
the long road out of town you have
to take before you can come back.

Sometimes I go trepanning for
gold, I give myself a secret name
& tell no one, so when I am jogging
past the radio telescope at dawn
and someone says, Hey ————,
I will know I am dreaming.

Sometimes I dream of bridges
wrought from elephant bone,
other exotic materials, heavy
metals, radioactive isotopes, or

I dream up headlines like
MARILYN MONROE CHEST X-RAY UP FOR AUCTION.

Sometimes I draw cosmograms,
maps of the universe writ in radio
waves, bridges crossing vacuums,
never water. I know what water costs.
My cosmograms depend on echolocation.
I broadcast ARE YOU READY & await reply.

NEW THEORIES IN HUMAN LIFE EXTENSION

> *I want to outlive the turtle and the turtle's father,*
> *the stone.*
> —Terrance Hayes

The modern dead travel by television
now, though radio would also do,
your electromagnetic echo perpetuating

down the halls of the universe. If this
brand of immortality (quote/unquote)
doesn't suit you, consider freezing

yourself, or at least your head. (Don't
use alcohol, which preserves the brain
but in which memory is miscible.) If

the thawing question troubles you,
try a few laps around the termination
shock at near-light speed. Come back

in half a decade, it'll be the year 3,000.
(The energy cost is steep.) If free's
what you want, consider the turtle

and his father, the stone. Head
to the edge of the ocean and wait
for a wave to wash them in, or better

yet, head to the edge of the world
itself, lean over to see the turtle
bearing his stone father the earth

on his back, and ask: Turtle, how
much time have I got? Stone, how
about twenty-four hours more?

AFTER ADAM

A stillness over the face
   of the water. Cranes remain
motionless. The air settles,

   colonizes the bowed spines
of pine, of cedar, of oak.
   The trees exhale, unheard in

the wide silence of the world.
   For once there are no voices,
humanity gone, as through

   a mirror, looking over
his shoulder as he goes, &
   vanishing down the many

paths to the world after men
   & the heavens fear neither
skyscrapers nor zeppelins.

   His fires burn out. Only the
stars are radioactive,
   trillions—the bubble image

of a thousand galaxies
   reflected & vanishing
in the distance, through mirrors.

Who could look on that & not
weep, not tear his clothes, his hair?
   Creation, so much larger

than we'd feared. Yes, then, better
   none remain, the garden of
the earth dimming toward twilight,

   shadows over the deep, the
partial darkness of water:
     & man, asleep, dreaming of air.

NOTES & ACKNOWLEDGMENTS

"Diagnosis" first appeared in *Best New Poets 2009*.

"After Adam" first appeared in *Colorado Review*.

"Copula" first appeared in *Third Coast*.

"Anatomy Lesson (i)," "Persistence of Memory," and "Golem" first appeared in *DIAGRAM*.

"Donor" first appeared in a slightly different form in *Cincinnati Review*.

"Open Heart Surgery" won the Duke University 2007 Anne Flexner Award in poetry. It first appeared in *Wheelhouse Magazine*.

"Panel on Borderland" first appeared in the *Massachusetts Review*.

"Anatomy Lesson (iii)" samples language from William James' *The Principles of Psychology* (1890).

"Ho*e (iii)" owes its imagery to Junot Diaz's *The Brief Wondrous Life of Oscar Wao* (Riverhead, 2007).

"A Satellite Sees Into Your Heart" borrows a line from Dan Chiasson's *Where's the Moon, There's the Moon* (Knopf, 2010).

This collection would not have been possible without the help of countless people. Special thanks to: Joe Donahue, for encouraging me from the start; Laura Duane, for being my first reader and editor; Ander Monson, for believing in *Vivisection*; Don Bogen, Natalie Giarratano, Jeb Livingood, Beth Marzoni, Donald Revell, and David Wolach, for their editorial support; Seth Abramson, Adam Eaglin, Cynthia Reeser, Anne Marie Rooney, and David Silverstein, for their generous time and insight; and, of course, my family.

COLOPHON

Text is set in a digital version of Jenson, designed by Robert Slimbach in 1996, and based on the work of punchcutter, printer, and publisher Nicolas Jenson.

ERIC WEINSTEIN earned his AB *magna cum laude* in English literature and philosophy from Duke University and is currently an MFA candidate at New York University. His poetry appears widely.

❦

NEW MICHIGAN PRESS, based in Tucson, Arizona, prints poetry and prose chapbooks, especially work that transcends traditional genre. Together with DIAGRAM, NMP sponsors a yearly chapbook competition. Eric Weinstein won the contest in 2010.

DIAGRAM, a journal of text, art, and schematic, is published bimonthly at THEDIAGRAM.COM. Periodic print anthologies are available from the New Michigan Press at NEWMICHIGANPRESS.COM/NMP.

www.ingramcontent.com/pod-product-compliance
Lightning Source LLC
Chambersburg PA
CBHW031420040426
42444CB00005B/660